BEGINNERS GUIDE TO CRYPTOCURRENCY

Since the inception of Bitcoin and Cryptocurrency about a decade ago, the technology
Have enjoyed a rapidly growing popularity across the globe not just because it`s a good store Of value but mainly because gives an edge against inflation thus, why it`s gradually replacing Fiat in today's world. The space have already attracted a lot of attention over a short period of time since its birth in 2009, with the majority of it supporters and adopters having little to no knowledge about the development. The aim of this material is to give a simple and easy to understand beginner`s guide to Cryptocurrency and Block chain technology.

TABLE OF CONTENT

BEGINNERS GUIDE TO CRYPTOCURRENCY

ALL RIGHTS RESERVED
CHAPTER1.
INTRODUCTION

CHAPTER 2
IT SUPPORTERS FOR THESE REASONS:

ALTERNATIVE COINS OR ALTCOINS

THE PROS AND KONS OVER CRYPTOCURRENCY
CHAPTER 3

CAUTION

PEER-TO-PEERFOCUS
NO BANK FEES
ACCESSIBILITY

SCALABILITY

CYBER SECURITY THREAT
PRICE VOLATILITY
REGULATIONS

FUNGIBLE TOKENS (NFTS).

CHAPTER 4
CRYPTOCURRENCIES WALLETS AND EXCHANGE

COPYRIGHT©2022GRACE HILLARY

ALL RIGHTS RESERVED

CHAPTER1.

INTRODUCTION TO CRYPTOCURRENCIES

BLOCK CHAIN TECHNOLOGY

Crypto currencies are digital assets intended to serve as a medium of exchange (e.g.

Money) in which individual records of coin ownership are kept in a centralized public ledger is called block chain.

I want to point this out and not just a form of money. Bitcoin was the first cryptocurrency

Developed in 2008 before later releasing it as the first decentralized system in 2009

Cryptocurrency, however over 10,000 other cryptocurrencies have been created since then the way any monetary system works, it needs a record keeping system or ledger, turns block chain technology into crypto currency. Block chain technology is one

Decentralized ledger technology that stores transaction records (blocks) in multiple databases

(Chain) in a network connected by peer-to-peer nodes. That means the block chain is a record book similar to that used by traditional institutions such as banks and other financial institutions

Institutions, except that it is a centralized and programmable network technology that saves data in blocks that are impossible to hack. The earliest work on block chain technology dates back to 1982; the first block chain was designed and implemented by Satoshi Nakamoto in 2008 a core component of the crypto currency bit coin the following year a public ledger for all cryptocurrency transactions

System emerged after the 2007 global economic crisis that shook the economies of most countries with high inflation rate and devaluation of local currencies as a result of

The government is printing more money to stimulate

these countries' economies to create a stable, secure and limited supply of money in order to gain an advantage over the already rapidly growing inflation rate, Satoshi Nakamoto created Bitcoin.

Crypto currencies and block chain technology have proven to be very popular and appealing.

CHAPTER 2

IT SUPPORTERS FOR THESE REASONS:

I. it is seen by its supporters as the currency of the future.

Ii It removes the management of the money supply from central banks and thus reduces inflation.

iii. Other supporters such as the technology behind crypto currencies, the block chain, because it is a decentralized processing and recording system and can be safer than traditional payment systems.

ALTERNATIVE COINS OR ALTCOINS

The term is used to refer to crypto currencies and other types of digital assets that are not bit coin. It is commonly used to describe crypto currency coins and tokens created after Creation of Bit coin.

The list of such crypto currencies can be found on the homepage of the

Web site of coin market cap .command coingecko.com.

THE PROS AND KONS OVER CRYPTOCURRENCY

Due to the uniqueness of decentralized digital currencies, there are some advantages

(Advantages) as well as medium advantages

(Disadvantages) for holding and trading in these digital currencies via fiat currencies ten years old, the land scape of digital currencies is constantly changing and always present new opportunities and threats for users.

CHAPTER 3

THEPROS: USER AUTONOMY

Bitcoin's primary draw informs users and is in fact one of the central tenets of Bit coin .Crypto currencies are generally autonomy. Digital currencies allow users more control about their own money as fiat currencies. Users can control how they spend their money without dealing with an intermediary authority like a bank or the government.

CAUTION

Crypto currency transactions are private unless a user voluntarily publishes their bit coin. Transactions of these purchases are never linked to his personal identity, similar to cash purchases and cannot easily be traced back to him. Address generated for user purchases changes with each transaction and greatly less tied to personal identity than some traditional forms of payment.

PEER-TO-PEER FOCUS

The cryptocurrency transaction system is purely peer-to-peer, meaning users are able to send and receive payments to or from anyone on the network around the world without require approval from an outside source or authority.

NO BANK FEES

Cryptocurrency users are not subject to the unnecessary traditional banking fees and excessive bank fees associated with fiat currencies and bank accounts. Account maintenance or minimum balance fees, no stamp duty or card maintenance fees no overdraft fees and no repayment fees, among others.

ACCESSIBILITY

Because users can only send and receive crypto currencies with a smart phone, computer is Bitcoin theoretically for user populations without access to conventional

Banking systems, credit cards and other means of payment

Banking services for the bank less.

THE DISADVANTAGES:

SCALABILITY

With the rapidly increasing number of digital assets and their acceptance, the block chain is now faces the challenge of handling the high influx of transactions. The Bit coin network for example is currently only capable of processing seven transactions per second, which is still dwarfed compared to the number of transactions made by payment giants like VISA and MasterCard processes per second. However, several solutions have been suggested, including Lightning networks and use of options to overcome the scalability problem.

CYBER SECURITY THREAT

Cryptocurrency will be subject to technological

development just like any other

Security breaches and can fall into the hands of hackers, as we have seen several

ICOs and exchanges are being hurt, costing investors hundreds of millions of dollars.

PRICE VOLATILITY

The cryptocurrency ecosystem has been called a bubble by many because the high price volatility, although this still offers some opportunities for some users pose a major risk to most people in space It is important to many that increased acceptance of crypto currencies should increase consumer confidence and reduces that volatility over time.

REGULATIONS

Until the technology is adopted and properly

regulated by governments at all levels, there will continue to be an increased investment risk due to the risk of the probability of governments banning crypto currencies and regulators formulating anti-crypto laws currently China and Nigeria are the largest economies in Asia and Africa

CHAPTER 4

NON-FUNGIBLETOKENS ANDCRYPTOCOLLECTIVES

Fungibility is the ability to exchange something or replace it with another item of similar value and still retains its original value, similar to fiats, gold, dollars, a movie ticket or even bit coin. For example, the value of a $100 bill is the same as the value of five $20 bills, so if you give me $100, I could choose to pay off that debt with $1 bills and it will still be acceptable

Attributes that distinguish it from other items of the same asset class and cannot be replaced or substituted in any other way that retains its original value. Take, for example, a work of art, a house, a brand, or a video game like crypto currencies, NFTs are digital assets that are publicly verifiable on the block chain except NFTs are mental properties like a piece of digital art, virtual land, and collectibles authenticated on the block chain. Unlike other crypto currency coins and tokens, NFTs are not interchangeable and constitute an immune representation of a physical person keep in mind that the Pokémon cards. In 2017, a Canadian studio Dapper Labs developed a game the ethereum network called Crypto kitties. This game allowed players to buy, collect, and farm and sell virtual cats and no kitty could be transferred or sold without the permission of the user as it is an individual the identity was verified via the block chain

FUNGIBLE TOKENS (NFTS).

(According to The New York Times Magazine, Le

Kitty sold for around $140,000)

Today, the NFT and gaming industries have grown into a multi-billion dollar industry with multiple

NFT projects and technologies are emerging. Both the gaming and art industries are showing strong use cases for NFTs, and while NFT is still in its early stages, there are many use cases for the technology and a promising future for tokenized assets

CHAPTER 5
CRYPTOCURRENCIES WALLETS AND EXCHANGE

Since the proliferation of cryptocurrencies and other digital assets, there has been increasing need for secured funds to store these assets and a readily available market to quickly buy and sell these digital assets wallet where you hold your investments, as well as the exchange where you trade them, like that choosing the right wallet and exchange is even more important than the assets you own trade with them. Keeping crypto assets in an insecure wallet can result in permanent loss of your own investment and therefore it is very important that you carefully choose which wallet and which one exchange to hold and trade these digital assets.

According to Wikipedia, a cryptocurrency wallet is a device, a physical medium, a program or a service that stores the public and/or private keys for crypto currency transactions. Just say that a cryptocurrency wallet holds cryptocurrencies and other digital assets kept for short- to long-term purposes, it may be software such as an application or a piece of hardware like a physical wallet. Crypto wallets are like your banks that store digital assets are stored and crypto currency transactions are carried out. To ensure the safety of assets, each wallet is protected by a unique pair of public and private keys. The public key or wallet address serves the same purpose as a traditional bank account number and is used essentially for transaction purposes, allowing users to make crypto deposits as well interact with the block chain. The private key, on the other hand, is more personal signature affixed to a bank account that grants only the account holder access to the funds saved in the account and control over the funds in a cryptocurrency wallet, which is why it is advisable never to share them Private keys with everyone.

The classification of cryptocurrency wallets has been done on different bases by different ones Individuals who focus on different traits in each attempt, however crypto currency wallets are roughly classified into custodial and non-custodial wallets before breaking down further into these different forms. A custodial wallet is a type of crypto wallet that stores the private key by a trusted third party (usually an exchange), where the third party is in control of the wallet while giving the user permission to send or receive payments as well as carry out other transactions from the wallet hold and trade their crypto currencies and other digital assets large amounts of crypto currencies when exchanging, but instead on private or hardware wallets, as assets held on exchanges do not belong to you while you are on the ex-change .In September 2020European crypto currency exchange platform ETERBASE was packed and is a result over $5.4 million worth of cryptocurrencies were stolen and never recovered. however, a non-custodial wallet is a type of cryptocurrency wallet in which both the public and private keys are held by the individual wallet holder, giving the holder complete control about the assets in the wallet. Just say that an custodial wallet allows users to own banks, it means users have full control over the funds on the associated wallet. Examples of this wallet include software/hot wallets, paper wallet, hardware wallet, and more other offline wallets.

CRYPTOCURRENCY EXCHANGE

A cryptocurrency exchange or digital currency exchange (DCE) is a platform that users to buy and sell cryptocurrencies and other digital assets to factor other digital assets. Crypto currency exchanges are similar to brokers in the forex market and the stock market, except that these brokers open the trading floor to their clients being able to trade local currencies and stocks against fiat, crypto exchanges basically allow users trade digital assets like Bit coin, Ethereum, Ripple, Binance coin, Tronanda and others.

Exchanges have played a crucial role since the early days of Bit coin matching crypto currency buyers with sellers. Without those forums that attract a global user basis, we would have much worse liquidity and there is no way we could rely on the correct price of one asset. Before the widespread growth of cryptocurrency exchanges, where and how to buy and selling bitcoin was a big problem as there was no readily available online marketplace for it people interacting on a global scale, people would normally meet on bitcoin to talk about popularity forum where cryptopunks interact at the time to find buyers and sellers for their bit coins. however, crypto currency exchanges are everywhere these days and offer different ways to do this users to trade their crypto currencies the transaction took place on Bitcoin, spoke to Laszlo

Hanyeczand paid 10,000 BTC (worth approx $41 at the time) for two large pizzas from Papa John. chooses the safest exchange to trade your bit coins and others crypto currencies are very important to avoid losing your entire investment. centralized players have dominated this field; however, with the rapidly evolving stack of available technologies, a growing number of tools for decentralized trading have emerged: Centralized Exchanges (CEX) are cryptocurrency exchanges with a central authority or a third party that gives users the floor to buy and sell cryptocurrencies and other digital currencies. Assets such as NFTs and tokenized shares, with all parties involved trusting this middleman for the proper handling of their assets create a profile and verify their identity by providing some personal information about themselves, this practice is similar to that of the traditional banking system, where customers trust the bank with confidential information about yourself and in return the bank keeps your money secure. Some of the well-known centralized exchanges are Binance, FTX, Kucoin,

Crypto.com, Okex, Bitmex and Bitfinex. Decentralized exchanges (DEX) are, with the exception of the hassle of signing up and verifying the account holder. In most cases there is no deposit or withdrawing crypto currencies. Trading takes place directly between the wallets of two users, with limited (if any) input from a third party. DEX allows direct interactions with the.

Block chain without the need for an intermediary. Decentralized exchanges can be a bit trickier compared to centralized exchanges and may not always have the assets you want, but as technology and interest in it continue to grow, they may well become an integral part constituent of the crypto currency space in the near future.

www.ingramcontent.com/pod-product-compliance
Lightning Source LLC
Chambersburg PA
CBHW050315220526
45465CB00005B/1999